D1520289

This book is dedicated to all the *little black boys* who felt like they weren't good enough.

Little Man Little Man,
Do you know how special you are?

Your skin so rich we see from afar

Little Man Little Man,
how tough, how strong

Your arms and legs they stretch so long

Little Man Little Man,
unique and brave

Your hair it locs, it twists, it waves

Little Man Little Man,
your eyes so bold

they sparkle and shine like blocks of gold

Little Man Little Man,
there's power in your tongue

Your word is your bond, no matter how sung

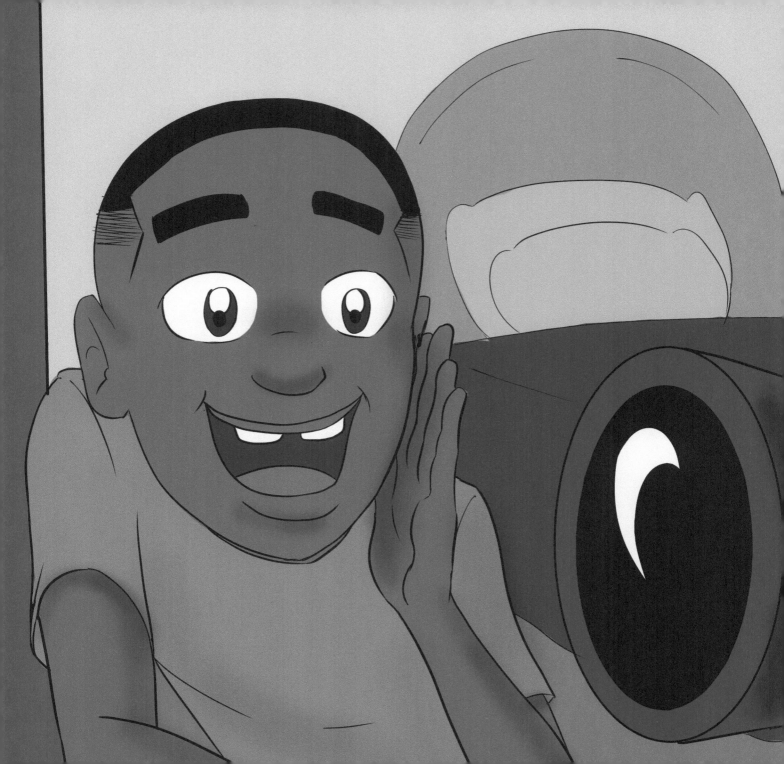

Little Man Little Man,
use your hands and feet

Be kind to all you love and meet

Little Man Little Man,
don't you ever fret

for life has joy you haven't seen just yet

Little Man Little Man,
don't you ever be afraid

to live your truth through life's parade

Little Man Little Man,
please reach for the stars

for only they and I know how special you are

Special Thanks

Thank you *God*, for choosing me to write these words, for giving me the creativity to design this book and for seeing it through. Your promises are truly yes and amen. I would also like to thank to my family and friends for encouraging me to publish this book. I couldn't have done it without you.

Lastly, I want to give a special thanks to my Pops.
I love you!

Skippy

CPSIA information can be obtained
at www.ICGtesting.com
Printed in the USA
LVHW071911210620
658649LV00021B/858